The Shamble

by
Steve Lambert

Close To The Bone Publishing

Contents

ONE | *The Fumbler*

TWO | *In Eynsham*

THREE | *The Shamble*

FOUR | *We Can't Resist*

About the Author

Steve Lambert was born in Louisiana and grew up in Florida. His writing has appeared in *The High Window* (UK), *Chiron Review, Saw Palm, New Contrast* (South Africa), *Northampton Poetry Review* (UK), *The Pinch, Broad River Review, Longleaf Review, Into The Void* (Ireland & Canada*)*, *Emrys Journal, Tipton Poetry Journal, Cortland Review*, and many other places. He is the recipient of four Pushcart Prize nominations and was a Rash Award in Fiction finalist. He won *Emrys Journal*'s Nancy Dew Taylor Poetry Prize. He is the author of the poetry collection *Heat Seekers* (2017), the chapbook *In Eynsham* (2020), the short-story collection *The Patron Saint of Birds* (2020) and the novel *Philisteens* (2021). He lives in northeast Florida, with his wife and daughter, where he teaches part-time at the University of North Florida.

Publishing Credits

Grateful acknowledgement is made to the editors of the following publications who published earlier versions of these poems:

SOFTBLOW: "The Fumbler"

The High Window: "The Boring War," "The Downturn," "The Birdfeeder," "Unbecoming," "At The Holiday Inn, Ashford, Canterbury Road," "In Canterbury," "In Stratford," "Banal Observations on Marital Longevity"

Chiron Review: "The Birdfeeder"

New Contrast: "Ars Poetica," and "Unbecoming"

The Pinch: "In Whitstable," "In Eynsham," and "My Wales"

Longleaf Review: "In St. Mawes"

Tipton Poetry Journal: "After Reading John Clare"

Northampton Poetry Review: "Honest John" and "Hamiltonesque"

Emrys Journal: "Serenade for Larkin," **winner of the Nancy Dew Taylor Poetry Prize**

Red River Review: "Comfort"

Eunoia Review: "Concerning Fatherhood and Self-destructive Tendencies" and "Concerning Feelings of Otherness with Nature and a Growing Numinosity"

Sky Island Review: "Stuck in Traffic on I-95 Southbound"

Haggard & Halloo: "Concerning Melancholy of Childhood, et al." as "How to Homebrew"

Saw Palm: "4.11.20"

"Hard Luck Lovers," appeared in *Endlessly Rocking*, an anthology of the Whitman 200 Project, published by Unbound Content, in celebration of Walt Whitman's 200th Birthday

"In Eynsham" also appeared in issue 39 of the *Eynsham Council & Community News* (West Oxfordshire, England, U.K.)

All poems in section two, except "In Dover," were published as a chapbook, titled *In Eynsham* (2020 CW Books)

For anyone who would...

The Shamble

ONE

The Fumbler

"…he barely hid his life…"
— **William Matthews**

In Praise of Anachronism

Braun is outmoded.
Muscles unstitched,
flap in the wind
like sheets on clotheslines.

I'm nostalgic for clotheslines,
for things of diminished utility,
like rotary-dial phones and cursive writing;
things with muscle, things
not useful in ways commensurate
with modern intentions.

Things like poems...

Hard Luck Lovers

Twenty-two years back
we're naked in a squathouse
living room. Our bodies

painted up like Woodstock
hippies—your breasts sunflowers,
my belly a sun—sway and tangle
as they bloom out of control.

We have nothing but ourselves
and what the other will allow,
too young and alive to be
anything but happy.

Gretel & Hansel

My brother cries often, needs help.
He says, "I think I overcooked this one,
Sister," when he calls one night after
getting drunk and taking the bus across
town to visit an alleged crack house.

"I wanted to see what one really looked like,"
he explains. My brother's like a poet:
he veers off, goes down dangerous
paths and, sometimes, needs help getting back.

"What did it look like, Little Brother?"
I ask. "It did not disappoint," he says.
"It looked just like a witch's hovel."

What else can I do? He's done
the unspeakable for me.
I will always help him back.

Ars Poetica

I come here often
and leave in various states.
I come here for answers
and I come here to parse the emptiness.
It may be emptiness itself, this place, like a dark cave.
I might fill it with suggestions of emptiness:
emptiness upon emptiness.
I might come here to make loud, echoey
pronouncements on emptiness.
Emptiness may not factor into it at all.
But it might. It's possible that nothing,
which is not emptiness, will happen here.
That is the more likely scenario.
It's important to remember that.
Let this be my only expectation.

Science Fiction

Who knows why?
The gods have all died
of natural causes,
not murder,
as originally thought.
Barring divinity,
what else?
Love's mundane,
an everyday
occurrence,
like death and birth
and flatulence.
Everything ordinary
seems strange
enough, likely
as extraterrestrials.
Love is
science fiction.

Kenneth Rexroth

Volume 160, Item 1462.
-University of Pennsylvania.
Photographs from the American Poetry Review Records,
1971-1998. Ms. Coll. 349.

In this photograph, a martyr's mournful face.

A lifetime of heavy sadness, expressed all at once,
weighs on this busted, sagging sandbag of a face.
It says that nothing is more distressing than the present,
not even death
—especially not death.

Is this how Job looked near the end,
his whole face given to the task of grieving
the loss of everything except his faith?

Is this what four failed marriages does to a man?

We're Killers, the Living

I remember the day:
a bumblebee,
like a bullet,
sent my father to the
emergency room.

He did not die,
but could have,
my gentle father,
who had already done
some of his own
light damage
to the world.

Heartless nature hides
death in its center
the way a child
hides a coin
in her sweaty palm.

All things
carry within
some undoing.

The Boring War

You sometimes hear a heart throb
or a groan of adolescent impatience,
but no real war cry. During a ceasefire
you venture in for a closer look: a carnage
of wrinkled clothes festoons her room,
and the illusive ache of loathing loiters
like teenagers at a convenience store
door. One long, sad love song on a loop,
the battle hymn of this untidy republic.
You remember a time when this realm
belonged to anyone who entered it,
a gleaming open society, not a Utopia,
but close, and as unreal as the unicorns
and fairies that inhabited it. This was no
war-torn outland. But daughters become
young ladies and may hate you for a while,
even if you painted this room ocean-blue
on request when she was eleven and
assembled the dollhouse that leans in
shambles in a far corner, a pink Grey
Gardens for hairless, one-armed Barbie
and naked Ken. Even if you were, as you'd
promised yourself you would be, nothing
like your own father and gave stability.
Stability was what you had wanted. But
what you did or didn't doesn't factor
into it. This is a feral land now, FTW etched
into a drawer of the monolith dresser.
The dialect a little different, with a subtle
Bite. "Daddy" has given way to "Dad."
Still nothing truly dangerous ever happens
here, only the occasional virginal shot at

promiscuity with a boy too shy, thank god,
and awkward to give her anything to fight for.

Ditch Digger

Fill this hole:

fill it with
fuck and feel dirt.
Fill it with
drink loam and eat soil.

Plant seeds
and bury treasures here,
in this hole.

Put a body in it—
it'll fit.

Fill this hole
with whatever you got;
throw it all in.

Dig it all up.
Do it again.

The Downturn

An interior decorator's eye is needed here,
or maybe just a sullen teenager
to paper the walls with glossy posters,
fill the room with languid cigarette smoke.

The light in here is slow and heavy,
almost stroboscopic.

Men and women sway silently in their chairs
like leaves of grey turtle grass in a cold current.
They're not, technically, dead.

It's true, they never let us forget,
Things could be worse.
"At least we have jobs" is cliché.

Even this dismal vision is diversion
from a dismal vision of life.
Even this monochromic horror is escape
from some other horror.

The Birdfeeder

She bought it and hung it
on a high limb of the loquat
tree in our back yard.

A blue jay came first, fat
and quick, and knew what
to do. Then two cardinals

flew in, an old married couple,
learned in the ways of birdfeeders,
and joined in. Then a lone dove

lit lovingly on a branch
just above the small menagerie
and studied how. This was

no performance, but
a kind of unselfconscious
laissez-faire avian harmony.

For a time, a calming rightness
reigned here—then the squirrel
came, seemingly from nowhere,

and jumped on top of
the feeder, scattering the birds
in a shockwave of birdseed,

as the feeder hit the ground
hard. I sat bemused in the aftermath

of its anarchy and watched
the tawny rodent forage.
I did not intervene, and,
in the right light, we all
got a little something.

May 2019

You must be middle-aged: quaint,
doting and mild; nostalgic, even,
always pining for anything intemperate
and wild. You change little from
year to year. But now I think you're
made of memories of Spring's madnesses.
You say, "I'm happy now, though I
didn't used to be, and will soon
be unhappy again," convalescing and
rehabilitating. You also say, "What
troglodyte doesn't care about the Moon
or the names of birds?" You are an
eighteenth-century English novel,
an epistle with too many characters
insincerely apologizing to each other,
idyllic scenes and digressions and rain.
Rain! I forgot the rain. May, let's not sell
you short. There's more to you, after all;
afternoon storms and insipid mockingbirds
that won't stop their ranting, like the time
our house mockingbird, perched on the
streetlight, wouldn't stop its incessant
mocking. A houseguest, between beer
sips, said, "Harper Lee has ruined the
damn creature for the rest of us. It's not
her fault though. She didn't know her
book would be so goddamn beloved."

The Fumbler

I

I'm building a ship in a bottle.
A study in frustration.
I'm called scatterbrained.
Presumably, there's no gun at my head.
But doing nothing isn't a choice.

II

We were lazy. We were "bad kids,"
truants and druggies.
I don't remember much.
"You're just misguided knuckleheads,"
said Mr. Ratley. We all liked him,
even Pete, the tough kid.
We hoped he was right.
I was short and chubby.
I studied Pete's clothes and his walk and his haircut.
(This is the first time I've admitted this.)
I turned around and he said,
"If you don't have a new haircut tomorrow,
I'm going to kick your fucking ass."
Most kids are cruel, some are mercenary.
I'm harrier now, and taller, but that's all.

Unbecoming

Florida, late summer, about to rain
or is raining or has just stopped. It's something
you come to terms with or love anyway.
Maybe it's why you're here, where
your divining rod has led you.

I've been learning how not to hate
for the last sixteen years, been learning
the rhetoric of love through immersion.

But they're lodged in me like a fossil fuel,
meanness and cruelty: so much accreted awfulness.
There's love, too, though, fathoms of it. I'm trying
to unbecome what makes me unbecoming.

We all go undiagnosed with some ill, and the rain
will never stop, only subside and come again, and,
anyway—don't you love a good deluge?

Rock Skipping

For H.

One wet Sunday when I was eight,
a few months before we'd learn
of you, Dad and I spent the day
together. He took me to Grecian
Gardens for breakfast and I ate
too much. After, we stood on the
bank of the Indian River, in view
of the crumbling green dragon.

"Who would you want to live with
if me and your mom were *apart?*"

I skipped that word across the
face of the river and considered
making a swim for it. Maybe I could
make it on my own, fend for myself

on a river islet. Eventually, I said both.
"One day with you, one day with mom.
One day with you, one day with mom…"
I held no concept of time beyond days.

They never divorced. Light damage
was done. A year later, you were pushed
into our cracked end of things, and
together, over the years, we've developed
a knack for skipping words at least three
times across almost any surface.

Beachcombing

All varieties of physical perfections and grotesqueries
here along the wet, ragged, foamyedge,
among the wasted and washed-up: he delights and
horrors of human flesh laid bare,
like bold offerings, amid these hard remnants of
hard lives who never drew a single breath, but instead
sucked and filtered and kissed life from undrinkable
waters.

TWO

In Eynsham

"Isn't it better, this wheeling…"
— **Richard Hugo**

At the Holiday Inn, Canterbury Road, Ashford

We arrive, airplane-travel weary, drink pints
of Carling in the courtyard out back where rabbit
shit dots the tuffets of green grass. The bar and dining
room grope in the shell of a sixteenth-century barn.

We are on our way to Canterbury
and on and on westward from there.

The rabbits, the size of Scottish Terriers, come out
in the afternoon and watch us drink, like the prelude
to an incursion, a scene from *Watership Down*,
but they keep their distance.

Behind the courtyard, beyond the leering rabbit mob,
one of England's many River Wyes dies down
to a murky piss dribble. This place is beautiful, but sad,
like a shrug before a sob.

Back inside Tommy, the young bartender, watches
us while his boss watches him spend too much time
with the Americans. The regulars give us "Slaughtered Lamb"
looks. "Wait," says Tommy when his boss disappears,
"you don't have Roundabouts in America?
How do you know where to go?"

In Dover

Tunnels are under us
for WWII spies
and gray clouds
above us. Wind
shoots the rain
like birdshot.
The White Cliffs
are just that.
Below the town,
a slick strip,
a main drag,
gritty and cramped,
but not the
"real shithole"
an old-timer in
Ashford called it.

In Canterbury

On the River Stour a college boy
walks upside down under a bridge.
Punters and rowers all around
tell the city's unofficial history:
ghost stories, pub brawls and crawls,
murders. The ghosts of black and grey
friars prowl the narrow streets
like night cats. I see a tall beautiful
young lady standing on the bulkhead
whose look is so distinct I try
to imagine her life but stop when
it gets too sad. She stands and lets
the human current rush around
the towering rock of her body.

In Whitstable

Asphalt-black fisherman cabins,
three-quarter size,
as if built for coastal Hobbits,
line the beach promenade.
To the East, the tarmac plant
hulks quiet as a dragon's horde.

English, if weather could have
a nationality: misty, grey and cool,
everyone seeming to walk
like characters from a spy novel,
hunched slightly forward,
hands in pockets, furtive glances…

Reserved delight creeps
into you like a fever
you want to have. The whole scene
reminds you of how boring
you find sunny perfection…

We walk in our mizzly daze
up Whitstable Beach, swerve left
onto Sea Street, where
the Prince Albert Public House
stands and waits, and is still waiting,
the only pub we pass
without entering, too much atmosphere
to drink in out here.

Back out at the water's edge
the English Channel spreads
wide and we watch ourselves
swim across, past the wind turbines,
to Calais and back, knowing
no one drowns. We want to live

here, but never will.
This Whitstable isn't real,
but the misty dream you have
of us in some place
we'd always rather be.

In Eynsham

For the Dandy Family

Eynsham, *West Oxfordshire, at the river Thames,*
midway between Oxford and Witney, sacked
by the Saxons in 571 AD, now a quiet civil parish.

I lie in a general
practitioner's
bed reading
a Simenon
Paperback.
A high window
in the hall
is open and I
pause to listen
to the low
warbling
complaint
("My toe hurts,
Betsy") of a
wood pigeon
and smell a
pleasant,
unnamable
something
on the air

as children
squeal, at play
in a nearby
Neverland: life
gently asserts
itself here

on this cool
afternoon in an
old, familiar country
whose architecture
dies now of old
age, or natural
causes, or it does
not die at all.

In Stratford

"Look," says the young man
in a tracksuit and a house-arrest anklet,
"Americans." His two friends
smirk at us. Next to a white Ferris Wheel
and willows with pageboy haircuts
that line the Avon, I consider
our conspicuousness. "Keep cool,"
I say to myself. "You don't want
to get your ass beat in Shakespeareland."

We walk down river
to the Church of the Holy Trinity,
where Shakespeare's buried.
"What's this," says Abi,
"the place where Sherlock Holmes
was born or something?" We say
things wrong on purpose.

Inside it's cramped. I can hardly
breathe, and it smells like age upon
age of ripe, shuffling humanity.
There's something distinctly
undignified about everything,
something tragic, Shakespearian.

In St. Mawes

Once, in Tampa, we made a drunken
habit of jumping off bridges into McKay bay,
where luminescent algae set our bodies
aglow. We looked like toxic merpeople.
But this isn't Tampa, and I almost drowned
in that bay, so I watch the jumpers, watch
my wife and daughter, Americans, and the
only ones in bathing suits, jump off the
ancient quay. My thoughts a hodgepodge,
I consider, oddly, how the Creature from
the Black Lagoon was filmed in Florida,
and is an iteration of Grendel, and how
intrepid saints have a fondness for banishing
serpents a' la Beowulf. Existence is an Ouroboros.
So you come here, and you jump, if you're
one for jumping, as I'm not. Mawes. Maudet.
Maudit? Cursed saints preserve us. Sometimes
a thing, a place, is defined by what it isn't.
Cornwall isn't England or Brittany or Ireland
or Wales. Across the harbor, in Falmouth,
is castle Pendennis. I'm always elsewhere.
In some towns even the locals look like tourists.
Strange that they have palm trees here,
in Cornwall, and saints you've never heard of.

My Wales

"...a place where it is lovely to die..."
– R.S. Thomas

Driving up from South Milton, Devon,
with its narrow roads like paths cut through
a wizard's maze, my allergies get so bad I consider
going to some English country doctor. This is middle
age, I decide, if you're lucky enough to reach it: slow
atrophy and physical discomfort. The radio reports
that a lorry has crashed, bleeding oil onto the M5,
so we call our hotel in Cardiff to cancel with no
refund, turn back toward Eynsham. It's true,
every day above ground is a good day, a victory,
but it's hard going sometimes, and I'll probably die
slow in some gleaming Florida hospital. It could be
lovely to die here, though, so close to Wales.
But we are usually laid to rest wherever
we come to rest, and it's the living that matters,
anyway, even in Wales.

After Reading John Clare

I sit on my back porch and listen
to the dreary weep of whippoorwills.

One calls close by, and another,
far off, seems to answer. I find it

almost irritating, the irksome way
this world signals to itself. I go in

and listen to the inside singing:
the dust-bunny hum of the fan in our

bedroom, the small-engine purr
of the cat on the couch, and the low

chatter of the night-watchman TV
in Abi's room. All worlds have their

ways. Time moves in cool swells
in this moment: so much is required.

Honest John

Composed with some lines (augmented) pilfered from Clare

The *evening's shadows creep in like leisure*
and put my mind at ease with things
that creep, or that seem to, John, Honest John.
After a life of hard work and dying children,
I wonder, *did the wind mutter at you*?
Did *distant fires blaze*? Did nightjars jar the night
free of nightmares. Did skylarks dart like bats?
Did you walk through the autumnal *grassy bent*,
past jack o' lantern Northborough, through the night,
along some span of bank on the River Nene
you called your *trickling sanity*, towards *the long
and lingering sleep we weary travelers crave.*

Wordsworth

Composed with some phrases pilfered from Wordsworth

We didn't make it to Tintern Abbey,
or the River Wye, because we didn't
make it to Wales. The geography
of Romantic poetry drops easily
from itineraries. But conjured up,
later, in *lonely rooms,* we can *see
into the lives of things* unseen.
It's impossible to understand, but
I love how we lovingly knock around,
looking for small Illuminations *in the fever
of the world* and, sometimes, find them.

Hamiltonesque

"Did I truly think that poetry, if perfect,
Could bring back the dead?"
   – Ian Hamilton

And who would you bring back?
And could you preselect the living?
Save someone from a death to come?

My dad comes to mind: my only
profound adult death to date.
My daughter for immortality.

The dead are not-so-secret
gods, if they want to be.
If that's a thing.

But who would you bring back?
Only one. How do you choose
without contributing to life's
ultimate, blazing indifference?

And who could write
a perfect poem, anyway?

Life's not fair. But death is—
is the only thing that is.

Serenade for Larkin

"Not to be here, / Not to be anywhere, / and soon;
Nothing more terrible, nothing more true."
    — Philip Larkin

One of the few things I dislike
about winter is how early
it gets dark out. Summer isn't better,
but its days linger at the end
the way the gravely ill do.
I don't agree with you, Phil, but I'd like to.
Night comes at the end of every day,
no matter the season. I'm okay
with big-d death, the *total emptiness*,
arrogant and true. We, all of us, die.
It's sad, but I'm fine with it,
the comfort of nothing.

Comfort

"He's one of these Englishman of the welfare state who writes self-effacing poems about how much he hates his record collection."
  − **James Dickey** on Philip Larkin, *Paris Review*

My office at night is a suitable salve.
My books lie about the shores of it,
like Eakins' bathers, self-effacing, cocksure,
my boxes of records hulk in its hollows
like impotent, tiresome haints. Like the prettiest
girl at school, a place has to mistreat you a
little before you can properly fall in love
with it. This modest space, tucked into a
labyrinth of blush-colored houses and
adolescent trees, feels like home now.
I've acquired a taste for the painfully innocuous,
have learned to appreciate the nuances of
ordinary, good like an English Bitter, and mild.

THREE

The Shamble

"…the tune your bones play
as you keep going."
— **Mark Strand**

"Life stands up all over the body like fine hair."
— **Betty Adcock**

"…the world's still false, cruel and beautiful…"
— **Charles Simic**

Finding the Right Geography

To achieve some emotional balance, live
close to moving water, a river, an ocean, a sea.
Lakes teem, crowded and empty, like graveyards,
nothing and everything underneath.

This ocean-cornered state, nearly drowned,
barely above water, is sufficiently positioned.
There's something about the constant threat
of submersion that puts a mind in the right place.

Concerning Water Moccasins and, As Such, Death

We were fishing with cane poles
at Green Swamp, on the Peace River
outside of Bartow in Polk County.
1988. As it struck up the bank at me,
my uncle seized it by the tail and
pulled down like a lion tamer cracking
a whip, killing it. A Moccasin's bite
can be deadly. The sudden violence
of that moment made me ill. Death
is there still. I'm not one hundred
percent sure this happened.

Glossolalia: *The Shamble*

"And then, again I heard the racket of crows,
Who were not gods…"
– Rodney Jones

August because August is fed-up,
with its visible bend up the tired road and baked-in
hellishness…
Yeah, it must have been August…

That morning, quotidian,
Detailed—then all at once,
            like a night terror…

Something grabbed hold of me, shook
shame and fear aloose,   minute glossy crows
that flew, that grew
as they lit about
            and bent like black monks all around—

crows as big as ravens.

        (Oil-spill-black wingnut grackles
        touched, too, and went among
        the crayon-black clacking crows.
        High, high above a swallowtail kite cut
        loose infinities through the sky.
        A hummingbird chased, maybe, a chickadee.)

Then it was quiet and…
time trekked in from far off, as if it came
from someplace primitive and harsh and had a
destination.

41

It was terrible and childish and Welsh
in design (everything was black and gray and a little bit
grim—and rainy),
and I decided to quit the pew and vaulted-ceiling shit.
There's an awe within it all
without that—and

It's a kind of secular blasphemy
to feel the hum and drum and clap
and still need any of it.

Then they whispered, the crows did,
like conferring defendants,
all at once,

and flapped
their raven wings as the jitters and jumps
                    settled in. I felt sublimely unspecific,
diffuse
…parts of me far away by ages
from the godawfulness of
                    those with no awe in them…

Yep. That morning something
neither evil nor holy
took hold—
        some drunken hobgoblin, not thought nor feeling—
laughed an aspect
into my bones and—I crave it always…
yet have it always.

I pour a drop of it out *here*…

A vision of a vision of…

All, I think, I ever needed, and
too much at times, and ugly
and how, maybe, animals and
newborn babies are,
a nearly unmanageable nostalgia
for total insignificance.

Remember that?
Have you been there and done that?
I can't say I recommend it…
A perfect fullness of emptiness swirling everything…

Dark matter maybe…endless depths of it…

then a beautiful tumult
like *the singing of drunken sailors…*

Then the *coos, caws, rattles and clicks* of Corvidae…
(Is this just some exotic personal heresy—
a self-portrait with birds…?)

No, it never did happen in April. That's for sure.
April *sucks.*
August is the cruelest month
and most terrible and primed
for this, late summer and burnt through
and nearly autumnal.

Then what? Hell if I know….
But, instead of angelic trumpeting,
instead of John Miltoning,
I *would* like it if the dead told jokes,
long and intricate and without
proper punchlines….Modernism
of the Netherworld or no world, no place,
nowhere.

Anyhow that's the godless scripture and theology,
the dogma of a crowded moment of
intuition and disengagement and *what all*:
primitive, significant, meaningless.
But its only partial—only a glimpse—
can never be figured in its fullness—
and I promise—I swear—
light pulsed through it all.

On Learning

I take things in rabid snatches.
Anything substantial I go at like a shark
at a hunk of meat. Once inside, fragments
seek each other out. They crave the whole
they were. They make their meaning
for me this way.

Concerning Fatherhood and Self-destructive Tendencies

Dad warned he'd never wake me
a third time on school mornings,
so when I resisted, could not bring
myself to rise and face those adolescent
days, he bombarded me with shoes
or rolled me out of bed with a lift and flip
of my mattress. Once, he poured
a pitcher of ice water the length of
my sleeping teenaged body. My father
was a lovely man but could not
suffer a boldface indifference to his
authority. So much goes unappreciated,
unheeded, unnoticed: *love's austere
and lonely offices.* But my dad was not
the common martyr. He craved
true tribulation, occasions to rise to,
or to be brutalized by, so he crafted
his own adversities, and overcame
them, and didn't, and kept going,
made a misadventure of his life,
and of ours. Anything to ward off
the anonymity of the ordinary.
The dull day to day was his ruin,
but he wouldn't let it be mine.

Concerning Feelings of Otherness with Nature and Growing Numinosity

Just below the Bible Belt
in the soul-heavy subtropics
I contrive a theology for myself.
This is the place for it, deep illusion,
has been for hundreds of years.
I shake dead leaves from trees
and eat exotic fruits off branches.
I make a quiet fuss of things.
I take to the piney woods at night
and run along the firebreaks.
I stray deep into the woods
and stay for a long time
unafraid of the dark or *God's will*.
I like the woods but not nature.
My blood feels like old,
soured civilization blood.
It's lonely here in the woods
and twiggy sounds break around me.
I leave here for someplace else,
someplace less alive, less holy.

Hangovers

An echo in the head, a loud, loose
Gatsbian blur. One or two crystalline
awkward Moments here and there.
Furtive glances of furtive things.
Excessive urination.
Random details. A glimpse
of an exceptional something,
A roaring red-lipped laugh,
foggy smoke around it all, a social
faux pas everyone decides to ignore
or postpone responding toout of a
collective dedication to the moment.
Some coarse joke taken a little too far.
Some opportunity, a lingering look,
not taken advantage of. Much gossip,
always. All things dressed down as casual
happenings, naked, purposeful accidents.

Universal Irreverence, i.e. Thumbing One's Nose at the Idea of God

Inexplicable everything...
You are given wide berth,
like a fire truck en route, but you keep going,
and everything burns...

The Big Whatever made whatever.
The dysfunctional bureaucracy
of things:

we politely die while you
lean on your shovel.

Ars Poetica

A verbal geometry of intangibles
Representations of
The cacophonous nature of actual
Thought processes
Or pre-thought
Removing the filter between internal
Mind crawl and experience
Verbal expression free of
Grammatical constraints
And syntactical obligations
Pure, unsullied Expression
But still meaningful
Especially meaningful
More meaningful
The most meaningful?
Not merely a dumping of
Psychic gobbledygook
Although that sounds interesting too
Rimbaud without the yelling
Dali comes to mind
But the temperament of someone
Like Edward Hopper
Kandinsky is even better
Nativism, naiveté
Primitive, Natural, intuitive
Non-representational
Cave writing
Being whatever it is
Unapologetically
Exploratory, limitless,
Free of expectations
Of correctness

Purely what it is
If it is anything
Purely

Concerning Melancholy of Childhood, et al.

I learned to ride at age four on a stolen bike
spray-painted policeman blue,
the sweetest thing with two wheels.
A nineteen-year-old neighborhood thief,
with the improbable name of Duper,
gave it to me. My wise mother,
not one to cross a budding criminal, thanked him,
smiled. When dad got home that evening they
consulted. I don't remember what they decided,
but I rode that ugly blue bike all afternoon.
Without knowing, I rode it like it was stolen,
a hot commodity. My only problem that day
was stopping. I didn't know how. I just rode
fast until I was tired and then slowed down
in the grass and fell over.

Concerning Things Kafka Said Better

This morning a shipwreck of choices.
Well, just get out of bed, for starters.
Objectively speaking, a first right choice,
Easily made. But from here it gets tricky.
The world, your small bit of it, encapsulates you.
Some of the people in it with you
need you, and, about that, all choices
have already been made.

Concerning Genealogy and Legacy

You have the blood for it.
Some ancestor fought you here.
You'd need to take from me.
Give me a handsome uniform to wear.
I'd bait the ladies with it.
For a farewell fuck
I'd pull your trigger.
I'd hate your enemy as well as you.
Give me a *purdy*
and I'll wear it proudly,
mount it on the wall when I'm old.
If I die young, at least I've lived.

Concerning Genealogy and Legacy, Continued

We sit in bars and parked cars
and around fires and lie to each other.
Each in turn tells his story. Beer helps.
Dad's got a doozy about a cousin,
a yellow-toothed inbred with a penchant for spitting:
how he hawked a green gob on him one morning
while they both sat in the bed of an old pick-up
on the way to work some groves,
and how he came off the wheel well
and kicked him upside the head,
sending the man overboard, to the ground,
and off rolling into a ditch, the truck just
barreling down the dirt road
through a grove of lemons.

Concerning the Demystification of Downtime

Jesus, visionary, lovely.
We let 'em get a hold of shit and they
fuck it all up. This was a six a.m. dreamy
note to self:

you wanna do something revolutionary
and politically significant?
Grow the fuck up.

Many of them have mental problems. So do
people with Mortgages and careers.

I dreamed last night of vinyl out of order,
LPs in chaos, and nobody cared.

I've heard that dreams are nothing more
than the mind working through possible
future scenarios—practice, as it were.
Mental fire drills. I hope that's bullshit.
It's dreaming without the dream!
Daytime's a glaring, beautiful nightmare.
I'll take my shuteye straight, please.

Banal Observations on Marital Longevity

Love is not self-sustaining.
Just ask your spouse who has hated you
more than anyone has ever hated you.
This is why you, Reader, must do, at least
occasionally, some rare thoughtful thing,
such as the for-no-good-reason flower purchase.
Fix it, whatever it is, before they ask.
Don't make them love you from scratch all over again.
Give them something to build off of.
It's a little work, is all. Love's a little work.

Early Middle Age,
Thoughts on Aging

I look closer now
As you age you slouch toward things
(Plus my eyes are going)
But I still miss a lot
I'm not expert at patience
And observation
Just because I've got some gray hairs
I'm still fucking up a lot of the time
But it doesn't bother me so much now
I'm an old only child
I don't even look wise

Stuck in Traffic on I-95 Southbound

The bumper sticker on the Jeep Rubicon
in front of you says, "Florida: A State of Mind."
Tell me something that isn't, you say
to no one. The cars on the left creep forward
half a car length and a KIA Sedona,
Rhode Island plate, packed with luggage,
two teenaged girls, and a small, serious
woman, hands ten and two, rolls by. It's
okay, you tell yourself, to let bumper stickers
be dumb. Delaware, a middle-aged man
driving a vintage corvette, stalks Rhode Island,
like a skeevy ex-husband. These are the people
going south with you—slowly going nowhere
with you. This time of year—for as long
as you can remember—I-95 fills up with cars
with Quebec plates. *Je Me Souviens*. Do you
remember? As a boy, on family road trips,
staring out the car window at their faces as
they passed, speaking a wordless French to
you, your face answering in its own dumb,
indistinct American English. Because we never
can be, we all want to be someone else.
But now you drive, are no longer a child.
You try to find affection for the routine,
the everyday, because you must. But you still
look for exotic faces in traffic. You know a
little French and Spanish, and, after four decades
of looking, understand faces better now.
You strain towards a provisional camaraderie
with your fellow motorists. You breathe deep:

Everything's work-in-progress. Every driver at least
feels essential, and your exit's only another three miles.

The Here and Now and Then

Shamble along. Change nothing…

Not who we *are*
just who we anxiously *were*:

innocence coming into knowing,
beautiful as hearts breaking.
Is hearts breaking.

That's life, somewhat.

Even if we do not live well, we are all,
eventually, brilliant at being dead,
which is something.

      The day-to-day
            a dull dance
      choreographed
            by our addictions
      and hard to do…

FOUR

We Can't Resist

"Here we are alone again."
— **Louise-Ferdinand Celine**

3.20.20
For Abi

Today you're seventeen.
We're afraid to go outside.
We let you go to the beach one last
time before "sheltering in place."
The world is changing,
our daily lives contracting.
There's nothing we can do.
But don't be sad on your birthday.
Right now, as always, love surrounds you,
like a protective spell, like a shield,
like a vaccine that works.

4.04.20

"...our feelings prey on us."
    – **Jane Austen,** *Persuasion*

All eras and epochs are
the worst there's ever been.

But to be confronted
so nakedly with ourselves...

The unvarnished truth
of our locked-in lives:

and the deceptions therein.

4.11.20
St. Augustine, FL

Here we are, god damn it,
nearly half a century in,

our lives just beginning to ache
in unromantic ways, old ways.

We're not supposed to touch
anymore but I can't resist.

We touch *each other*, yes, but
it's our own faces we can't resist.

I never realized, you say,
how often I do it. I've touched

mine so many times in forty-five
years I'm sure I've sculpted it,

pressed it into its present shape
and dimension. It isn't the work

of a master but it has its charm.
Such is my way even now: a fool

too in love with everything to take
the time to learn any *one* thing.

May 2020
For Keri

I sit and watch her in the garden
out back: She grows
fruits and vegetables:
various pumpkins and muscadines,
tomatoes, sweet and hot peppers,
things you can grow in Florida.

She does not grow flowers.
*I want to grow what
we can eat,* she says.
Not every seed planted
will grow.

*I had walked
through gardens all my life
without seeing them,*
had no use for them.
Now there's nowhere
else to go.

So she waters and waits
a patient waiting. I venture out
and watch her write in water
what cannot be said.

She is the garden I see.

Nature is a Nihilist

With William R. Soldan

Count the days and reckon
the distance like this: the buried
dead from the living dead.

Tomorrow is just today, again.
Every poem could be titled "Sisyphus."

Nothing matters unless you want
it to. No one these days knows how
to proceed, so we tune in for our
next move, watch the dog of indecision
nip at the hooves of a cold black
horse; play in the fields of our former
lives, while, best we can, we carry
what little light is left to where we
need it most. In this story, the mask
is not a metaphor, not in this language.
We don't speak anymore, as the
silence stresses the edges of this
space we've never quite filled.

Gratuities, Apologies, Explanations, Excuses, and Errata...

1. Epigraph for section one is from the William Matthews poem, "Babe Ruth at the End," from his book *Time & Money*.
2. The poem "Kenneth Rexroth" is an ekphrastic poem based on a photograph of Rexroth I saw on the *American Poetry Review* website. His face in this photo is a mask of deepest anguish.
3. The epigraph for section two is from the Richard Hugo Poem, "Shark Island," which appears in many places, including Hugo's *Making Certain It Goes On*.
4. The epigraph of the poem "My Wales" is a misquote based on my misreading of R.S. Thomas' poem "Come to Wales." The original line is "...a place where it is lovely to lie." I love and respect Thomas and his work. But I couldn't help letting the misquote stand.
5. In the poem "The Holiday Inn, Ashford, Canterbury Road," the phrase "*Slaughtered Lamb*" is taken from the name of the pub in the beginning of the movie *An American Werewolf in London*.
6. Some of the phrases in "Honest John" are pilfered from several John Clare poems.
7. The italicized lines in "Wordsworth" are from William Wordsworth's poem "Tintern Abbey."

8. The epigraph of "Hamiltonesque" is from the introduction to his *Collected Poems*.

9. The epigraph for "Serenade for Larkin" is from Philip Larkin's poem "Aubade," as is the italicized phrase "total emptiness."

10. The *Paris Review* excerpt for the epigraph of the poem "Comfort" is from *The Art of Poetry No. 20*, wherein James Dickey disparages his better, Philip Larkin.

11. The three epigraphs for section three: 1. From Mark Strand's poem "Lines for Winter," from his *Selected Poems*. 2. From Betty Adcock's poem "Visit to a Small Mountain," from her book *Walking Out*. 3. From Charles Simic's prose poem beginning with "Dear Friedrich…" from his book *The World Doesn't End*.

12. The epigraph of "*Glossolalia: The Shamble*" is an excerpt from a Rodney Jones poem, one I can't seem to track down with any amount of "Googling" or searching through the Jones books on my bookshelf.

13. The italicized phrase in the poem "Concerning Fatherhood and Self-destructive Tendencies" is from the Robert Hayden poem, "Those Winter Morning's," a lyric that is, to my mind, the closest a poem can come to perfect.

14. The epigraph for section four is the first sentence of Celine's novel *Death on the Installment Plan* (trans. Ralph Manheim).

15. The epigraph for the poem "4.04.20" is from Jane Austen's novel *Persuasion*, which my wife and I read together while in quarantine.

16. The italicized portion in the third stanza of "May 2020" is taken from the Gerald Stern poem, "Gold Flower."

Printed in Great Britain
by Amazon